Hansel & Gretel

A Nightmare in Eight Scenes

HANSEL & GRETEL

a nightmare in eight scenes
by

Simon Armitage

This edition first published in 2023
by Faber & Faber Limited
The Bindery, 51 Hatton Garden
London, EC1N 8HN

First published in 2019
by Design For Today
88 Emmanuel Road, London, SW12 0HR
www.designfortoday.co.uk

Printed by DZS Grafik

A CIP record for this book
is available from the British Library

ISBN: 978-0-571-38445-7

faber

2 4 6 8 10 9 7 5 3 1

HANSEL & GRETEL

THE CAST

In order of appearance

◼ .... Father

◼ .... Mother

◼ .... Gretel

◼ .... Hansel

◼ .... Witch

◼ .... Swan

Illustrated
by
Clive Hicks-Jenkins

Scene the First

The boy was called Hansel.
The girl was called Gretel.

Hence the title: Hansel and Gretel.

The father cut wood. He was a woodcutter.

(Excuse me – carpenter, joiner, cabinetmaker)

Wood for the fire, wood for the oven,
wood to repair the roof
every time it shuddered.
Hard to cut wood when there aren't any trees.
When there are only splinters and stumps.
When the wood's on its knees.

And the mother made bread. She was a bread maker.

(Beg pardon – caterer, pastry chef, master baker)

Bread for breakfast, bread for supper,
bread without jam, bread without butter.
Hard to bake bread without yeast or flour.
When there's only cinders and stubble.
When the shelves are bare and the shutters are down.

So the boy was called Cold,
the girl was called Hungry,
right down to the bone,
from Monday to Sunday.

See:
Where there was once a village there was mainly rubble.
And where there was fun there was largely trouble.
And where there were kites there were mostly rags.
And where there was bunting there were chiefly flags.
This flag one week. The next week another.

Scene the Second

Hansel and Gretel
at night in their bedroom.
A bunk bed. He had the upper.

No she had the top.
No he had the top.
No she had the top.
No he had the top.
No she had the top.

Ah, they loved each other
like sister and brother.

At night they listened.
Listened to the sky.
Listened to the hills.
Put an ear to the keyhole
or a cup to the wall.
Listened to the father.
Listened to the mother.

And you know what it's like when you're eavesdropping
when you shouldn't, when you're ear-wigging
when you mustn't.
Like sound underwater,
like an old radio,
all whisper and rumour.

This from the father:
My heart bleeds for those kids.
We can't feed or clothe them,
can't treat or school them,
can't give them a future.
We need to hide them where bombs can't find them.

And this from the mother:
They're not safe in this house.
I keep dreaming a dream:
if they lie here they die here.
We need to lead them away and leave them
if we really love them.

So what the kids received as plotting and scheming
was sobbing and weeping.

And what the parents believed was snoring and dreaming
was fretting and grieving.

Lower the bucket into the well
and there's nothing but sludge,
but now a small tear like a silver snail
that was thought extinct
comes crawling from Hansel's eye.

Boys don't cry.

Pump the pump
and turn the tap
and it coughs up dust
or hiccoughs dirt
or vomits rust,
but now a tear like a priceless diamond
comes sliding down Gretel's cheek,
a trembling, shining blob.

Girls don't blub.

Day drags itself under the threadbare blanket of night,
day calls it a day and closes the great door of the dome of night,
day rolls over and faces the wall, the wall of night
riddled and pock-marked and punched
by the sniper rounds and bullet holes
of planets and stars,

the full moon
like a doodlebug through a barn roof.

Gretel finally cries herself to sleep in Hansel's arms.
Except Hansel's arms are somewhere else,
in the sleeves of his coat,
his feet in his boots,
his legs on the move,

his hands like pink tarantulas crawling down tracks and paths,
going from place to place,
gleaning pebbles that wink or shine,
pocketing stones till his pockets are full.

Then reaching up,
his arm now like a giraffe's neck
or a telescopic elephant trunk
(he's never seen an elephant, or a giraffe,
except in the dog-eared leaves of a charred book)
to where a neighbour's fresh white loaf cools on a windowsill.

It's theft, but needs must.
And not for eating, even if
a starving hyena prowls in his gut, even if
a shiver of ravenous sharks patrol his blood, even if
his belly thinks his Adam's apple's been lopped.

Scene the Third

It was a full day's hike.
It was a two-day trek.
It was a three-day slog.
It was a four-day trudge.
It was a five-day yomp.

Then:
Here's a good place.
Let's take five.
Let's make a camp, build a fire.
Kids – get some kip, some shut-eye.
Bed down like hedgehogs in a nest of leaves
below the sycamore's eaves.

And the mother says:
Why can't we stay
with the little ones –
boy of my bone
girl of my womb –
make a new house
under these thick limbs,
under these strong boughs?

And the father says:
They're safer here –
boy of my spleen,
girl of my heart.
We need to go back
to our patch of earth
to defend what's ours.
Blood will find its way home.

And the mother says:
The woodcutter's son
will be safe in the wood,
among timber and trunks.
He knows how to fence and thatch,
knows his lime from his oak,
his birch from his beech,
his ash from his mountain ash,
his box from his maple,
his elm and his hazel;
which bends and burns
which hardens with age
which keeps out the rain.
It's there in the grain.

And the father says:
The baker's girl
should be at ease in the world:
she knows how to forage and grub
for flowers and nuts,
knows her seeds and fruits,
her tubers and roots,
her berries and bulbs,
her mushrooms and toadstools
her leaves and her veg.
As sure as eggs is eggs
she'll get by.
It's there in her eyes.

So under the green umbrella
of hornbeam and willow
and aspen and alder
and spindle and elder
and blackthorn and buckthorn
and on through the vigil
of standing larch and silent pine
they wave their silent goodbyes,
tread softly away …

a five-day yomp,
a four-day trudge,
a three-day slog,
a two-day trek,
a full day's hike.

We were right,
says Gretel, waking up.
Left.
Discarded.
Abandoned.
Cut off.

We're stuffed.

What food was left was only a raisin or two.
What fire was left was only an ember or so.

So it's true,
says Hansel, looking around.
Lost.
Rejected.
Deserted.
Dumped.

We're screwed.

What light was left was only a glow-worm's low-energy bulb.
What drink was left was only a foxglove thimble of dew.

I miss our room.
I miss our floor.
I miss our roof.
I miss the door.
I miss the window,
miss the walls.
I miss the mice.
I miss the fleas.
I miss my bed.
I miss my bunk.
I sleep on top.
No you don't.
Yes I do.
No you don't.
Yes I do.
No you don't.

I'm cold.
I'm hungry.
I'm thirsty.
I'm scared.
If we ever get back
you can sleep on the top.
Do these forests have wolves?
Do these woods have bears?

Then a cloud slid away
and out came the big white stone of the moon.
A great big boulder of light.

Hansel punches the air:

Oh stone is attracted to stone, says he,
and white is attracted to white, says he.
That's nothing but drivel and shite, says she.
No it's science and fact, says he – you'll see.

So I dropped these stones on the way, says he,
and now they're a luminous road, says he.
Oh I love you, you geeky nerd, says she.
These cat's eyes will usher us home – follow me.

Which was great.
Which was fine.
The moon winked
and the pebbles winked back.

Which was good.
Which was nice.
Till dawn broke
and the moon yawned and went out.

Now what, oh genius brother of mine?

Hansel punches the air:

Oh I knew the moon wouldn't last, says he,
so I snaffled a loaf of bread, says he.
But a loaf of bread's not a torch, says she.
But it kind of is, says he - you'll see.

So I crumbled it up on the way, says he,
and now we just follow the crumbs, says he.
A road made of bits of bread, says she?
Yes a road, and a road we can eat – follow me!

Which was great,
which was fine,
and they tracked the trail
for a couple of miles.

Which was good,
which was nice,
but foxes eat crumbs
and so do mice.
and so do birds.
In fact birds are especially fond of bread,

be it bloomer or farl
be it sourdough or scone
be it teacake or bap
be it soft or stale.
Be it rook or crow
be it wryneck or snipe
be it jackdaw or jay
be it coot or kite.

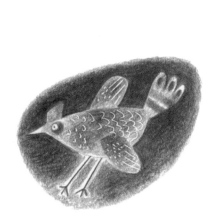

Blackcap. Whitethroat. Redstart. Wren.
Griffin. Harpy. Phoenix. Hen.

Sun up, the dawn chorus,
a million birds all looking for breakfast,
the road of crumbs well and truly digested.

Every portion pecked,
every titbit necked,
every morsel snecked
by twenty-past eight.

Gretel: Oh brother.

The morning sours into afternoon,
stagnates into evening,
curdles to dusk.

The forest a Garden of Eden by day,
full of earthly delights.
But a horror film after dark
and a ghost train at night.

Animal noises like swear-words and threats.

Ponds like eyes.

Marsh gas like strangers' breath.

Trees like kidnappers.

Pigeons like spies.

Twigs like fingers.

Dew like saliva.

Vines like snares.

Brambles like barbed wire.

Cobwebs like hair.

SUGAR!

They'd scented it on the breeze a mile or so back,
tasted it in the air, thought they were going mad.

SUGAR!

They'd followed the whiff like a long thread
reeling them in, hooking them forward, ahead.

SUGAR!

He thought it was a pan of bubbling caramel,
she thought it was burnt fudge or marzipan.

SUGAR!

It led them up and over a humpback bridge,
its spine arched like a hissing cat,
its keystone made of chocolate bricks,
the stream underneath flowing with fizzy pop.
On the other side the soil underfoot
was pure cocoa powder and nothing but.

SUGAR!

(Not that they'd had very much of the stuff. Hardly any at all. Where they came from it was rarer than gold or plutonium, more expensive than saffron or mobile phones, worth more than the local currency, kept in bank vaults under lock and key, sold by dodgy dealers on street corners, licked from the stomachs of dancing girls by gangsters and racketeers, buried in secret locations, ransomed for millions. Even the emperor or president or shah or sheriff or whatever his name was that week could afford no more than a single granule per day, which he placed on his tongue at dusk, and the sight of the sun going down and the sudden sweetness melting into his mind made him weep every time. I'M EXAGGERATING but the point is this: Hansel and Gretel were kids and kids go loopy for sugar and here was an actual THEME PARK of the stuff and an INTERACTIVE theme park at that!)

This is a dream.

A mirage.

We're tired.

We must be asleep.

Need something to eat.

Light-headed.

Low blood sugar.

Try one of these.

They followed a trail of small white balls,
not pebbles this time
but hundreds of shiny mints
that snaked through a garden
of Parma Violets and Cherry Lips,
past bushes and shrubs
whose fruits were Black Jacks and Sherbet Dips,
past flowers and plants
whose petals were Love Hearts and Percy Pigs and Foam Shrimps.

Foam Shrimps – remember them?

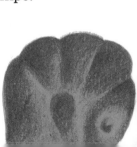

And arrived at a building – amazing –
with sugar-glazed windows
and liquorice fall-pipes
and toffee tiles
and brandy-snap gutters
and Chupa Chup chimneys
and Mars Bar lintels
and nougat walls
and a butterscotch door …

Oh sweetness, sweeter than sweet.
The psycho-candy doing its work,
across the tongue and into the gut
(Oh it's good, it's so bloody good)
and through the roulette wheel of the heart
and around the race course of the veins
and into the sweet spot of the brain
(Oh God, it's insane, it's truly bloody insane).

But you know what they say?
No such thing as a free lunch. No gravy train.

Children, this is your lucky day.
Children, children, tell me your names.

I'm Hansel.
You're most helpful.

(The boy's as thin as a streak of piss.
Too scraggy to haul and lift,
too weak to put in a full shift.
I'll fatten him up, give him some heft.)

I'm Gretel.
I'm most grateful.

(The girl's a bit on the dumpy side.
Too broad in the beam to catch the eye,
too podgy to fetch the best price.
I'll starve her, bring her down to size.)

You're welcome.
You're both welcome.

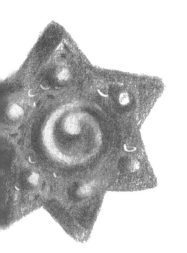

(In fact – two birds with one stone:
she can wait on him hand and foot,
run around, cook and skivvy,
slave till she's skinny,
fetch and carry, wear the pinny,
work off a few pounds.
And he can loaf and lounge,
nosh and trough and guzzle and scoff,
get some bulk and ballast under his belt,
pile on a few stones,
put some flesh on his bones.)

Help yourself to the yard and garden,
nibble and chomp all you like
then turn the handle
and come inside –
even the furniture's made of sweets.
Then you can wallow
in marshmallow pillows
and edible sheets,
dreaming your sweet dreams.
("Sweet" dreams. Geddit?)

But for candy-floss read spider's web.

And for chewing gum read super glue.

Read bird lime, fly paper, moth to a flame.

Drool over sugar, it turns to a thick, slow, syrupy goo.

Hence Hansel and Gretel
stuck to the house by their paws.
Stuck by their tongues to a door.

THERE NOW
FOLLOWS
A SHORT
INTERMISSION

CONFECTIONERY OF EVERY
CONCEIVABLE SHAPE AND SIZE
AVAILABLE IN THE FOYER
(BUT AT WHAT PRICE?)

DON'T BE SHY, LADIES AND
GENTLEMAN, GIRLS AND BOYS

DON'T BE COY

Scene the Fifth

Four weeks going by. Four weeks of this:

Empty crab shell for you, girl, profiteroles for the boy.

Empty crab shell for you, girl, tiramisu for the boy.

Empty crab shell for you, girl, pecan pie for the boy.

Empty crab shell for you, girl, lemon meringue for the boy.

Empty crab shell for you, girl, treacle tart for the boy.

Empty crab shell for you, girl, chocolate torte for the boy.

(I feel sick)

(I'm not done yet)

Empty crab shell for you, girl, mint chocolate chip for the boy.

Empty crab shell for you, girl, six Walnut Whips for the boy.

The boy in the cage, that is.
like a sad budgerigar.

The girl going nowhere fast,
like a mouse on a hamster wheel.

The slave-driver cracking the whip,
do that, do this, don't do that, don't do this.

Monster.
Witch.
Bastard.
Bitch.

I heard that.

Her ears were good
but not her sight. Practically blind.
Glasses like milk bottle bottoms.
Glasses like core samples of ancient Antarctic ice.

Empty crab shell for you, madam, sticky toffee pudding for the boy.

Empty crab shell for you, young lady, black forest gateaux for the boy.

Every few days she comes to the cage.
Stick your finger out, son,
let's see if you've made the weight,
let's see if you've plumped up.
Stick your pinkie out, lad, let's see what you've got!

But out through the bars
comes a chicken bone
or a hawthorn twig
or a drinking straw
or length of string
or a plastic pen
or a wooden peg.

Well fuck my old boots
what the hell what the hell I've pumped him with butter and eggs
and primed him with sugar and full fat milk and the rest
and he's still pipe-cleaner thin
as mean as the wind
as lean as a reed
still as spare
as a chicken bone
or a hawthorn twig
or a drinking straw
or a length of string
or a plastic pen
or a wooden peg what the hell what the hell's the matter with him?

She'll cut her losses. Take the hit.

Build a fire, girl, and rig up the biggest cooking pot.
Get the water lovely and hot.

She was only thinking of scrubbing him up.
He might be a runt
but better a pristine runt when she auctions him off.
She'll flog the sister as well,
get the pair off her hands, they'll sell as a job lot.

But no smoke without fire thinks Gretel.
Why the kindling and why the cauldron?

For bath she hears

For bathe she hears

For brush she hears

For soap she hears

For scrub she hears

For fresh she hears

For oil she hears

. . . broth.

. . . baste.

. . . braise.

. . . soup.

. . . grub.

. . . flesh.

. . . boil.

For
heat
she
hears
meat.

She hears **eat.**

Better act fast
or it's Hansel porridge,
Hansel hash,
Hansel potage,
Hansel goulash,
Hansel and mash.

Is the water ready, you silly goose?
    But Gretel plays dumb.
Did your mother teach you nothing at all?
    But Gretel keeps schtum.
So not just ugly but stupid to boot.
    Gretel doesn't move.
Lean over and dip your elbow in.
    But Gretel just shrugs.
I'll show you how but just this once.
    Then Gretel shoves.

And Gretel, let's not forget,
was a cook's daughter at heart,
and she knew about sugar and heat.

So in went the Drumstick lollies and White Mice,
the Rhubarb and Custards and Traffic Lights,
the Pear Drops and Wine Gums and Milk Teeth,
the Blue Dolphins and Flumps,
the Flying Saucers and Strawberry Chews,
the Chocolate Limes and Pineapple Chunks,
the Liquorice Allsorts and Aniseed Twists,
the Glacier Mints and Jelly Beans,
the Whistle Sticks and Midget Gems,
the Jelly Babies (for ironic effect).
And out went the fire, till the whole sugary globule
had cooled and set.

Till the job lot was a big glass fist
with a certain someone caught in its grip.
With a certain someone locked in its keep,
entombed for all time in a big boiled sweet.

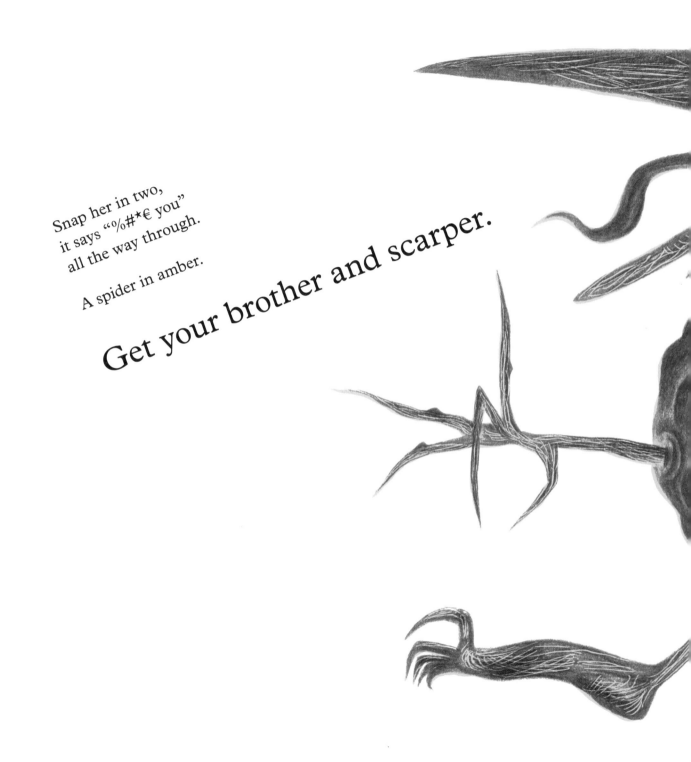

Snap her in two,
it says "%#*€ you"
all the way through.

A spider in amber.

Get your brother and scarper.

Scene the Sixth

But not before
a squint through the blinds.

A shufti, a gawp
just to see what it's like.

Kick down the door
and step inside.

House where the dark broods
House where the dark blooms
House where the dark breeds
House where the dark breathes

House where the light blinks
House where the dark seethes
House where the light squints
House where the dark glares
House where the light dares
House where the dark stares
House where the light swabs
House where the dark blots
House where the light slides
House where the dark hides
House where the light tries
House where the dark lurks
House where the light pries

House where the dark hurts
House where the light finds
House where the dark forms
House where the light falls
House where the dark clots
House where the light spills
House where the dark spoils
House where the light toils
House where the dark tells
House where the light sheds
House where the dark shades
House where the light masks
House where the dark basks
House where the light leads
House where the dark leans
House where the light peeps
House where the dark leaks
House where the light bleeds
House where the dark weeps

Gretel:
It's wrong to steal
but this silver spoon
reminds me of home.
And I won't say no to a chocolate coin.

Hansel:
It's wrong to thieve
but I love this knife
in its leather sleeve.
And I'll help myself to a chocolate coin.

Scene the Seventh

A full day's hike.
A two-day trek.
A three-day slog.
A four-day trudge.
A five-day yomp.

Still lost.

The woodcutter's son
with his stolen blade
slashing through canes and creepers.

Spoon in her hand
the baker's daughter,
spooning out honey and nectar.

Still lost.

In the ink of the night
they come to a ledge
and stop and stand
where the edge of the land
meets a watery void,
then wait on the brink
of some unknown drink
which might be a ditch
but might be a stream
and might be a river
but might be the sea.

Hop on
said a mute swan!

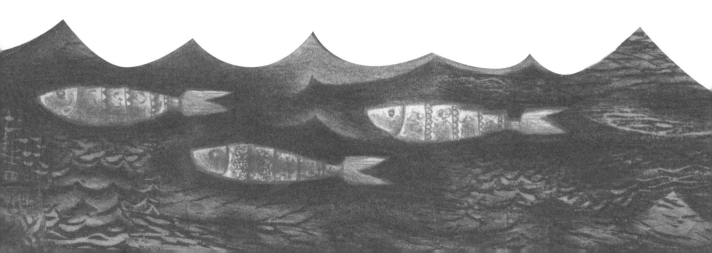

It wasn't there, then it was.
Like a seat on a carousel.
Like one of those fairground rides.
Like one of those pleasure boats on a boating lake.
Like one of those bedside lights
in the shape of a swan.
And it shone.

Hop on
said the mute swan.
I can take more than one.

For just a sovereign
I'll sail you across.
That's all it will cost.

So Gretel stumped up her chocolate coin and scrambled aboard.

That's a sovereign *each*.
Not a penny less. Up front, and in cash.

So Hansel coughed up his chocolate coin and clambered aboard.

And the world tilted and rocked, wobbled and rolled.

Question: when is swan not a swan?
Answer: when it's a rubber duck.

Question: can a rubber duck carry two on its back?
Answer: it can not.

Question: when is a rubber duck not a rubber duck?
Answer: when it's a leaky boat.

Question: can a leaky boat sail all the way to the far shore?
Answer: not sure.

Question: what was the weather like in the channel that night?
Answer: gale force seven or eight.

But Hansel used his knife as a rudder
and Gretel's spoon made a decent paddle

and they steered and rowed till land
emerged
      resolved
            declared
                  appeared
                       arrived

like new morning on the far side.

Scene the Eighth

A road picked out
by glisten and glint,
by glimmer and shine,
not pebbles or crumbs this time
but the shucked shells
of bullets and bombs
and torn off buttons
and broken medals
and lost buckles
and buckled metal
and twisted cars
and ruptured girders
and crazed ceramics
and littered shrapnel
and fractured armour
and shattered glass
and scattered parts …

that led to a pile of stones
that was once a home.
And a husk of a man
sitting there on his own.

A shadow of a dad.
But no mum.

She was knelt in prayer
by your empty bunks
when heaven delivered
a thunderbolt.
When a payload fell.
When an air strike struck.
And the hole it punched
in the rock-hard earth
made a sort of grave.
And what was left
of two small bunks
made a coffin of sorts.
And a rough wooden cross.

And the father weeps:
What man is this
who abandons his kids,
whose wife sleeps
in a makeshift box,
in a shallow plot,
whose estate is dust?

But the woodcutter's boy
was a chip off the old block.
And the cook's girl was the kind of fruit
that doesn't fall far from the roots.

There's this place –
it's a full day's hike,
a two-day trek,
a three-day slog,
a four-day trudge,
a five-day yomp –

it's a horror film after dark
and a ghost train at night:

animal noises like swear-words and threats,
ponds like eyes,
marsh gas like strangers' breath,
trees like kidnappers,
pigeons like spies,
twigs like fingers,
dew like saliva,
vines like snares,
brambles like barbed wire,
cobwebs like hair …

But a garden by day,
where the oaks stand thick and deep and tall,
where the figs hang sweet and ripe and low,
where lumber will roll
and seeds will shoot
and rain will be rain
not bursts of flame.
And if all else fails
there's this chocolate house, this gingerbread hall …

Come.

Come.

And they each picked up a small white stone as a souvenir

and moved on.

Acknowledgements

Simon Armitage's poem of *Hansel & Gretel* originated as the text for a performance work commissioned and developed by Goldfield Productions. It was directed and designed by Clive Hicks-Jenkins, and premiered at the 2018 Cheltenham Music Festival prior to a tour. Later recorded by BBC Radio 3 at the Milton Court Concert Hall, Barbican, the performance was broadcast on December 22nd, 2018.

Special thanks to Louise Heard at Benjamin Pollock's Toyshop for her inspiration and passion for the Toy Theatre.

Special thanks to Laurence Beck for colour and design work on Clive Hicks-Jenkins' artwork and book layout.

Designed and published by Design for Today in 2019. Winner of the V&A Illustrated Book Award in 2020.

Production credits for the 2018 tour. Music Matthew Kaner; Poetry Simon Armitage; Director and Supervising Designer Clive Hicks-Jenkins; Produced by Kate Romano for Goldfield Productions; Dramaturgy Caroline Clegg; Narrator/Singer Adey Grummet; Puppeteers Di Ford and Lizzie Wort; Music performed by Goldfield Ensemble; Puppets Jan Zalud; Puppet Wardrobe Supervison Oonagh Creighton-Griffiths; Models and Collage Phil Cooper; Paper-cuts Peter Lloyd; Animation Clive Hicks-Jenkins assisted by Phil Cooper; Model and Animation Camera Pete Telfer of Culture Colony Vision; Mixer and Stage Camera Jon Street of the Moth Factory; Lighting Design David Abra; Stage Management Andy Shewan.